My Little Book of
Monster Trucks

Chris Oxlade

Quarto is the authority on a wide range of topics.

Quarto educates, entertains and enriches the lives of our readers—enthusiasts and lovers of hands-on living.

www.quartoknows.com

Design and editorial by Starry Dog Books Ltd
QED Project Editor: Ellie Brough
Picture Researchers: Sarah Bell, Ewout Buckens

Copyright © QEB Publishing, Inc. 2017

First published in the United States by QEB Publishing, Inc.
Part of The Quarto Group
6 Orchard, Lake Forest, CA 92630

A CIP record for this book is available from the Library of Congress.

ISBN 978 1 68297 300 4

Printed in China

Words in **bold** are explained in the glossary on page 60.

Contents

What Are Monster Trucks?

Monster trucks are amazing machines. Many of them have the body of a **pickup truck** with huge, monster tires.

<< **This monster truck's tires are almost as tall as the driver!**

˅ Here is a monster truck in action, jumping and crushing cars!

Some people like to build their own monster trucks and then race them against other monster trucks. At shows, the trucks do jumps, **wheelies**, and other amazing tricks in front of big crowds.

» A visit to a monster truck show is a great day out for fans.

Monster Truck History

The story of monster trucks began in the 1970s, when several pickup truck owners in America started showing off their driving skills. One of them was named Bob Chandler.

>> Here's Bob Chandler mud bogging in his original pickup truck.

135 PAUL AVE. FERGUS

The truck owners tested their trucks by pulling heavy weights. They also enjoyed mud bogging—driving through deep muddy puddles!

^ Bob's 1970s pickup truck became one of the first monster trucks.

N,MO 63135   1 314 524-5113

MIDWEST
four wheel drive
CENTER

Bigfoot

Just for fun, Bob Chandler turned his 1974 pickup truck into one of the very first monster trucks! His friends named it Bigfoot.

« Bob gave his pickup bigger wheels and a more powerful engine.

>> In 1982, Bob built Bigfoot 2. Here it is having some giant wheels fitted.

<< Over the years, Bigfoot monster trucks kept getting bigger!

Bigfoot was the first 4x4x4. That means it had four wheels, the engine turned all four of them, and all four wheels steered the truck.

USA-1

USA-1 was one of the first generation of monster trucks built in the 1970s. Its owner, Everett Jasmer, was one of the original creators of monster trucks.

⌃ The original USA-1 was a Chevrolet K-10 pickup truck. Everett Jasmer made many changes in order to add the big wheels and tires.

⌄ **A radio-controlled model of USA-1 was made, based on the full-size truck.**

⌃ **This is Everett Jasmer, one of the first people to do tricks in monster trucks.**

USA-1 was built by Everett Jasmer. Everett owned his own truck parts business. He was a skilled **mechanic**, so he knew how to convert an ordinary truck into a monster truck.

King Kong

King Kong was another of the first monster trucks. It raced against Bigfoot, USA-1, and a truck called Bearfoot.

>> Owner Jeff Dane used parts from army trucks and tanks to build King Kong.

King Kong is most famous for a crash! In 1990 it was racing the truck Caroline Crusher when it flipped, rolled, and burst into flames. Fortunately the driver was unhurt.

⌃ There has been more than one King Kong truck. Here is Awesome Kong II doing a wheelie!

Wheels and Tires

What turns a truck into a monster truck? It's the wheels and tires. They're enormous!

⌃ Tractor tires were used on the first monster trucks.

Sometimes the tires are even taller than the driver! They have a chunky pattern, or "tread", which grips well when the truck is climbing over **obstacles** or driving through mud.

« The squishy tires help to give a soft landing after a jump.

>> Normal wheels and tires are used to drive monster trucks to a different place.

www.santapod.com

A Strong Frame

⌄ This truck has a chassis made of steel tubes. It is very strong.

The main part of a monster truck is its frame, or **chassis**. All parts of the truck are attached to the frame.

« The part of the chassis that surrounds the driver is called a **safety cage**.

>> The safety cage protects the driver if the truck rolls over.

In modern monster trucks, the chassis is specially designed for big wheels. A lightweight body is fitted to the chassis.

Springy Suspension

A truck's **suspension** system connects the chassis to the wheels. It includes **shock absorbers** that smooth out the impact of bumps.

« Big suspension springs let the wheels move up and down.

>> Pairs of wheels are connected by a long metal bar called an axle.

R1P BF

Axle

The suspension lets the wheels move up and down as the truck hurtles over obstacles and bumps. It also helps the truck to land softly after doing jumps.

<< This monster truck is landing after a big jump. Its front suspension is squashed!

19

Car Crushing

In 1979, Jeff Dane's monster truck King Kong crushed some old cars for fun! In 1981, Bob Chandler did the same in Bigfoot.

ʌ **Here is Bigfoot crushing cars for the first time.**

>> In 1982, Bigfoot crushed cars at the Pontiac Silverdome in Pontiac, Michigan.

A person who organized truck shows asked Bob to crush some cars at a show. Soon Bigfoot was crushing cars in front of big crowds!

<< Car crushing is still a popular event. Here is the monster truck Podzilla crushing a heap of cars.

First Monster Truck Races

Soon after car crushing became popular at shows, monster trucks began racing against each other along muddy tracks.

« USA-1 was one of the earliest monster trucks to race.

Bigfoot and USA-1 battled each other in one of the first monster truck races in 1983. Millions of viewers saw the race on a TV show called *That's Incredible.*

ᐱ **Here is Bigfoot kicking up dust as it tries to win a race.**

Truck Racing Shows

In the 1980s, monster trucks started racing each other regularly at monster truck shows. Racing is now a part of most shows.

Monster trucks sometimes race side by side along short, straight tracks. They roar away from the start. The first one to the finish line wins points, and sometimes prizes!

⌄ Sometimes trucks race over jumps and other obstacles.

⌃ Here are two monster trucks leaving the starting line of a race!

Driving Safely

It takes lots of skill to drive a monster truck safely! Drivers practice doing jumps and other tricks for hours and hours.

« The harness straps are connected to the frame.

Underneath a truck's bodywork, there is a strong safety cage that keeps the driver safe if the truck rolls over. The driver wears a safety harness to stop him or her from falling out of the seat.

Accidents Happen

Monster trucks are powerful vehicles, and sometimes even the best drivers have accidents.

<< Trucks can bump into each other during high-speed races.

A truck can tip over if it goes around a corner too fast, or if it lands awkwardly after a jump. Drivers practice getting out of overturned trucks as quickly as possible.

Mud Bogging

Mud bogging is another exciting sport for monster truck drivers!

⋁ **The trucks, and often the drivers, end up covered in mud.**

⌃ **Here's Bigfoot 1 racing through deep mud at a mud-bogging event.**

At a mud-bogging event, drivers try to steer their trucks through deep mud without getting stuck. Some get through, but others don't make it.

>> Here's a very muddy monster truck coming out of a deep mud bog.

Equalizer

Equalizer was built in 1988 by Gary Cook and David Morris. It won them the TNT Monster Truck Racing Championship in 1989.

⌃ **Equalizer's driver wears a suit that matches the truck's paintwork.**

⌃ You can see Equalizer's strong springs as it jumps through the air.

The first monster trucks had suspensions with leaf springs, which were very strong, bendy metal strips. Equalizer was the first truck to have huge **coiled springs** instead. They let it land more gently after jumps.

Swamp Thing

Here comes Swamp Thing. It's a monster truck painted to look like an alligator from a swamp!

> ⌃ Swamp Thing's front has a row of scary-looking alligator teeth!

This truck was originally called Dragon Slayer and was built in 1994 in the United States. An English driver named Anthony Dixon bought it in 2002 and turned it into Swamp Thing.

⌃ **Swamp Thing appears at monster truck shows all over Europe.**

⌃ **Here's Swamp Thing about to land after jumping over old cars.**

Modern Bigfoot

Bob Chandler, the man who built the original Bigfoot, has built many more trucks. They are all named Bigfoot!

« **Bigfoot 8 was the first monster truck to have a chassis made of metal tubes.**

Each new Bigfoot is given a number. The newest Bigfoot is Bigfoot 21. Bob Chandler is working on the next model, Bigfoot 22!

⌃ Bigfoot 21 was launched in 2015. It is a particularly loud monster truck!

Freestyle!

Monster truck fans love seeing jumps, wheelies, and **donuts**. These tricks are all part of freestyle trucking.

>> Freestyle tricks show off the skills of the drivers. Here's the truck Big Pete leaping through fire!

<< Obstacles in freestyle include old campers and pyramids of cars, vans, and buses.

Freestyle started in the 1980s, when drivers of early monster trucks began showing off their skills. Freestyle is now an event at many monster truck shows. The winner is decided by judges, or by how loud the crowd cheers!

⌃ **Here is Bigfoot, the original monster truck, performing a spectacular jump.**

Freestyle Trick:
Jumps

Jumping was the first monster truck freestyle trick. Jumps started small, but now trucks do enormous jumps!

<< The truck Tail Gaitor is taking off from a ramp made of dirt.

^ Crunch! Samson has just landed. Its front suspension and tires are squashed.

^ Here's Bigfoot flying through the air mid-jump.

To make a jump, a driver speeds up a dirt ramp and the truck flies into the air. If the driver gets it right, the truck lands on all its wheels. Sometimes trucks bounce into the air again after they have landed!

Freestyle Tricks:
Wheelies and Flips

A wheelie is a trick where a truck lifts its front wheels and balances on its back wheels. When it flips, it somersaults backward and lands on its wheels!

« Podzilla is doing a wheelie on top of some old cars!

To do a donut, the driver **accelerates** and steers hard to the left or right. The spinning wheels push the back end of the truck around while the front stays in the center.

<< The truck's chunky tires make circular skid marks in the dirt as it spins around.

A Monster Truck Show

A monster truck show is a great day out! It takes a lot of preparation to be ready.

<< The show organizers build dirt ramps for jumps and set up old cars to crush.

>> Fans can meet the drivers and take photographs of the trucks.

^ This truck is called Big Pete. It's performing in front of a big crowd!

All the action takes place in an arena. Fans watch from the stands as trucks race, crush cars, and do freestyle tricks. Sometimes the trucks do mud bogging and **truck pulling**, too.

47

Monster Truck Shapes

Most monster trucks look like pickup trucks, but some look like cars, vans, or even dinosaurs!

<< This monster truck has tracks instead of wheels.

>> The monster truck Big Pete is the shape of a truck cab.

^ Jurassic Attack even has horns like a *Triceratops*!

Most monster truck bodies are made from a material called **GRP**. Truck builders can make it any shape they like. Some truck builders use bodies from other vehicles instead.

Paintwork

Many monster trucks have detailed paintwork to make them look more exciting. The name of the truck is always painted on the side, too.

« The decoration on Monster Medic includes a one-eyed monster medic!

Monster truck owners like to paint their trucks in bright colors. Roaring flames, terrifying monsters, country flags, and superheroes are all popular on monster trucks.

≪ **Monster Medic is decorated in strong colors from bumper to bumper.**

Wacky Monsters

Some monster trucks aren't trucks at all, but they are still monstrous!

COOL BUS

<< Backdraft Wheelie is an old fire truck converted into a monster fire truck.

There are no rules that a monster truck must look like a pickup truck. Some monster truck enthusiasts have built monster machines from other vehicles instead.

∨ **This monster truck is a limousine. It can be hired to take people to parties!**

∧ **Here's a big yellow monster school bus doing a jump!**

Tank Track Trucks

Some monster trucks have **caterpillar tracks** like a tank. The tracks travel well over rough ground and obstacles.

« The body of this monster tank lifts up at the front so the crowd can see the driver.

» This monster tank has a pickup truck body fitted to tank tracks.

The monster tank Armour Geddon has heavy metal tracks that help it to climb over piles of old cars. The tracks are turned by the truck's powerful engine.

« Armour Geddon is called a monster tank because of its tracks.

Radio Controlled

Radio-controlled (RC for short) monster trucks are amazing toys that work by remote control.

« An RC truck can be controlled from a distance using a handset.

The driver starts, stops, and steers the truck with mini wheels and sticks on a remote control handset. With lots of practice, the truck can be made to do jumps, wheelies, and even flips.

hpi-racing

Record Breakers

Monster trucks hold some incredible world records. Here are two amazing examples!

« Bigfoot 5, the world's tallest monster truck, has tires as tall as an African elephant!

XD SER
like no other

In 2013, Joe Sylvester from the USA set a world record ramp jump in his monster truck Bad Habit. He took off up a ramp and landed 237.5 feet (72.4 m) away—that's three-quarters the length of a football field!

∧ **Here is Bad Habit performing its amazing world-record ramp jump!**

Glossary

accelerates Gets faster.

car crushing A monster truck event where a truck drives over old cars, crushing them flat.

caterpillar tracks Strong loops made from heavy metal pieces joined together.

chassis The strong frame that supports a truck's body.

coiled springs Springs made of a metal rod twisted into a coil shape.

donuts Monster truck tricks where a truck spins around and around on the spot.

GRP Short for glass-reinforced plastic, a strong material made from plastic that contains short fibers of glass.

mechanic A person who builds cars or is skilled at fixing broken cars.

mud bogging A monster truck event where trucks drive through deep, gooey mud.

obstacles Dirt ramps, piles of cars, or other things that a monster truck drives over during a race or a show.

pickup truck A small truck with a cab and an open back, often used by farmers and builders to move things.

safety cage A strong cage that keeps a driver safe if the truck crashes.

shock absorbers Parts of a truck's suspension that stop the truck's suspension springs from squashing too much.

suspension Parts of a truck that connect the chassis and the wheels.

suspension springs Strong springs in the suspension of a truck that lets a wheel move up and down.

tanks Military vehicles with tracks, a big gun, and armor to protect the crew.

truck pulling A monster truck event where a truck pulls a huge weight as fast as it can.

wheelies Tricks where monster trucks or other vehicles lift their front wheels into the air.

Index

Picture Credits

(t=top, b=bottom, l=left, r=right, c=center, fc=front cover, bc=back cover)

Alamy
8/9 © picturesbyrob, 14 bl © blickwinkel, 15 br © picturesbyrob, 16 bl © Buzz Pictures, 20/21 © Mim Friday, 25 r © Michael Doolittle, 26/27 © Michael Doolittle, 32/33 © PCN Photography, 35 r © David Wheeldon, 46/47 © Mim Friday, 57 br © Radharc Images.

"BIGFOOT"® and "SNAKE BITE"® are registered trademarks of BIGFOOT 4x4, Inc., 2286 Rose Ln., Pacific, MO 63069 U.S.A. © 2017 All rights reserved.
1, 4 bl, 6/7, 7 tr, 8 bl, 9 tr, 20 bl, 21 tr, 22/23, 30/31, 36 bl, 36/37.

Big Pete Ltd
18 bl Karen Shutler, 19 tr Colin Morgan, 26 bl Karen Shutler, bc tr & 38/39 Courtesy of SMA photography – Sean Atherton, 48 bl Courtesy of Armour Geddon, Karen Shutler, 49 tr Courtesy of Armour Geddon, 54 bl Courtesy of Armour Geddon, 54/55 Courtesy of Armour Geddon, Karen Shutler.

Ross Z. Bonar, TheMonsterBlog.com
32 bl, 33tr, 58 cl.

Jeff Cook, International Monster Truck Museum, WildmanJeff.com
14/15

By kind permission of Jeff Dane / Rudy Calooy of Killeen TX (King Kong)
12/13, 13 tr.

Fotolibra
bc c & 55 tr © David Hudson.

Frankish Enterprises/Don Frankish
48/49.

Getty Images
5 r © The Washington Post / Contributor, 30 bl © Barcroft Media / Contributor, bc ct & 31 br © Barcroft Media / Contributor, 47 tr © OLI SCARFF / Stringer, 53 br © Brad and Jen Campbell / Barcroft Media / Contributor.

Everett Jasmer © 2017 USA-1 4x4, www.usa-14x4.com
10 bl, 10/11, 11tr, 22 (Danny Maass/Maass Media).

Jeff Luckey (jeffluckeyphoto.com)
58/59.

Danny Maass/Maass Media
17 tr, 18/19, 22bl (by kind permission of Everett Jasmer), 28 bl, 28/29, 33 tr, 40 bl, 40/41, 42/43, 44 bl, bc bl & 44/45, 45 tr, 46 bl, 50 bl, bc br & 50/51, 52/53.

Samson / Dan Patrick Enterprises Inc
16/17, 41 tr.

Photoshot
56 bl © Photoshot.

Rex/Shutterstock.com
29 tr Justin Downing/REX/Shutterstock, 34/35 Terry Harris/REX/Shutterstock, 39 r Alan Simpson/REX/Shutterstock.

Santapod
bc tl, 2 Roger Gorringe, 4/5 Dan Smith, 24/25 Roger Gorringe, 38 bl Dan Smith, 42 bl Darren Skidmore.

Shutterstock
fc & 34 bl © Pavel L Photo and Video, 52 bl © Steve Mann.

Traxxas
Image courtesy of Traxxas. Used with permission.
56/57.

With thanks to:
Anthony Dixon for permission to use Swamp Thing.
Rich Blackburne at http://rtbracing.weebly.com/ for permission to use Monster Medic.
Big Dawg Monster Truck Racing LLC for permission to use TailGaitor, © TailGator www.bigdawg4x4.com

We would also like to thank all the featured trademarks for their kind help and for granting us permission to feature their trucks in this book.